A Very First Poetry Book

compiled by John Foster

Oxford University Press

OXFORD

UNIVERSITY PRESS

Great Clarendon Street, Oxford OX2 6DP England

Oxford   New York
Auckland   Bangkok   Buenos Aires   Cape Town   Chennai
Dar es Salaam   Delhi   Hong Kong   Istanbul   Karachi   Kolkata
Kuala Lumpur   Madrid   Melbourne   Mexico City   Mumbai   Nairobi
São Paulo   Shanghai   Singapore   Taipei   Tokyo   Toronto

with an associated company in Berlin

Oxford is a trade mark of Oxford University Press

First published in hardback 1984
Reprinted 1993

First Published in paperback 1984
30 29 28 27 26 25 24 23

A CIP record for this book is available from the British Library

Illustrations by Jan Lewis, Ingo Moore, Joe Wright

also in this series:

A First Poetry Book
A Second Poetry Book
A Third Poetry Book
A Fourth Poetry Book
A Fifth Poetry Book
Another Very First Poetry Book
Another First Poetry Book
Another Second Poetry Book
Another Third Poetry Book
Another Fourth Poetry Book
Another Fifth Poetry Book

ISBN 0 19 916050 3 (paperback)
Phototypeset by Tradespools Limited, Frame, Somerset
Printed in Hong Kong

Contents

Humpty Dumpty went to the moon

Humpty Dumpty went to the moon
on a supersonic spoon.
He took some porridge and a tent
but when he landed
the spoon got bent.
Humpty said he didn't care
and for all I know
he's still up there.

Michael Rosen

Clumsy

My sister
  trips
      over any old thing
          while giving
            the loudest
                of squeals;
                over shoes,
                  over mats,
                  over chairs,
                  over cats,
                    and finally
                        head over heels.

Max Fatchen

These are the clothes that my big brother wore

These are the clothes that my big brother wore,
And his elder brother,
And *his* brother before.
These are the short pants which reach to the floor,
For I'm much much shorter, than the brother before.

This is the hat, that he no longer wears,
For he has big brothers, and now he wears theirs,
And the socks I put on, are in non-matching pairs,
And the jumpers have sleeves full of patches and tears.

Yes, this is the sole of my big brother's shoe,
His big brother wore it, and *his* brother too,
And my Mum said 'My boy, I shall give it to you.
It's an honour to walk, in your big brother's shoe.'

These are the clothes that no rag man would buy,
With holes that have holes through which seagulls could fly,
But I wear them and wish it was not always I,
Who's the youngest young brother, and the smallest small fry.

Clive Riche

Paint on my fingers

I banged a nail,
I hit my thumb,
My brother laughed.
But not my Mum.
My brother tried,
To paint a space,
The paint went splattering
On his face.
He turned around,
And began to cry.
My Mummy laughed,
And so did I.

Clive Riche

10

Cousin Jane

Yesterday my cousin Jane
Said she was an aeroplane,
But I wanted further proof –
So I pushed her off the roof.

Colin West

Snore-a-bye daddy

Snore-a-bye daddy
In your arm chair
No one will wake you
No one would dare.

Under your newspaper
Worn like a wig,
Till we wake you at tea-time
You can snore like a pig.

John Kitching

Questions

I often wonder why, oh why,
All grown-ups say to me:
'When you are old and six foot high,
What do you want to be?'

I sometimes wonder what they'd say
If I should ask them all
What *they* would like to be, if they
Were six years old, and small.

Raymond Wilson

13

Crayoning

The sheet of paper is white
And perfectly quiet
Like a drift of snow
Into which nobody goes
And out of which nothing shows.

Then I crayon a sun to shine
And the sky's blue line,
A red house with a green door
And a chimney above it all
Out of which the black smoke pours.

In the garden is a mother
Hanging out clothes of every colour;
And flowers of every colour grow
Where once the paper
Was white as snow.

Stanley Cook

14

At Sea in the House

When I pretend them to be
The tables and chairs are land
Where you can safely stand
And the carpet between is sea.

The dining table makes a boat
And I climb on there
By way of the rocking chair
And out to sea we float.

The pattern in the carpet
Swims like fish on the floor
And anyone opening the door
Is sure to get very wet.

Stanley Cook

15

You were the mother last time

'You were the mother last time.
It's my turn today.'
      'It's *my* turn.'
'No, *my* turn.'
      'All right then, I won't play.'
'Oh, go ahead then, *be* the mother.
It's not fair.
But I don't care.'

'I was the father last time.
I won't be today.'
      'It's your turn.'
'No, *your* turn.'
      'All right then, I won't play.'
'Oh, never mind, *don't* be the father.
It's not fair.
But I don't care.'

'I was the sister last time.
It's your turn today.'
      'It is not.'
'It is so.'
      'All right then, I won't play.'
'Oh, never mind, *don't* be the sister.
It's not fair.
But I don't care.'

'I have an idea!
Let's *both* be mothers!
(We'll pretend
About the others.)'

Mary Ann Hoberman

17

I had no friends at all

I had no friends at all
Until you came my way
And now we play and play
All day. I only hope
You never have to go away.
It would be sad
To lose the only friend
I've ever really had.

John Kitching

18

Skipping rhyme

Netball
Setball
I had a soaking wet doll

Netball
Letball
Her name was Rosie Letfall

Netball
Getball
I threw her in the river

Netball
Wetball
I fished her out for dinner

John Rice

Sometimes

Sometimes
when I skip or hop
or when I'm
    jumping

Suddenly
I like to stop
and listen to me
    thumping.

Lilian Moore

A clear day and a yellow sun

A clear day and a yellow sun –
Oh, come with me and have some fun.
There is your shadow by your side;
Now run away and try to hide;
Run –
Out of breath all down the street,
And still your shadow's by your feet.

Gregory Harrison

I have to have it

I need a little stick when I
Go walking up the street,
To poke in cracks as I go by
Or point at birds up in the sky
Or whack at trees we meet.

I need a stick to zim along
The fences that we pass;
I need a stick for dragging through
The gravel or the grass.

My father says there cannot be
A single doubt about it:
I have to have a stick with me.
I cannot walk without it.

Dorothy Aldis

Flutter by

I chased it round the garden.
I chased it down the street.
I chased it to the river.
That's where I wet my feet.

I chased it over cowfields.
I chased it low and high.
I don't think that I'll ever catch
That dratted butterfly.

Seamus Redmond

The Digging Song

In your hands you hold the spade,
Feel its well worn wood.
Now you drive it in the earth,
Drive it deep and good.

    Dig dig digging dirt,
    Dirt inside your vest.
    Dig dig digging dirt,
    Digging dirt is best.

Soon your hands are red and raw,
Blisters on the way,
But your spade just wants to dig
All the long, hot day.

    Dig dig digging dirt,
    Dirt inside your vest.
    Dig dig digging dirt,
    Digging dirt is best.

Wes Magee

Little John was not content

Little John was not content
Unless he played with wet cement.
    One day alas in someone's yard,
    He stayed too long and set quite hard.
His mother didn't want him home
So now he's just a garden gnome.

Max Fatchen

A busy day

Pop in
pop out
pop over the road
pop out for a walk
pop down to the shop
can't stop
got to pop

got to pop?
pop where?
pop what?

well
I've got to
pop round
pop up
pop in to town
pop out and see
pop in for tea
pop down to the shop
can't stop
got to pop

got to pop?
pop where?
pop what?

well
I've got to
pop in
pop out
pop over the road
pop out for a walk
pop in for a talk ...

Michael Rosen

26

I don't want to go up to bed

I don't want to go up to bed.
I want to watch TV instead.
It's true, as you say,
That it's been a long day,
But I just don't feel tired in my head.

I know that I've cried and I've cried,
But now I am really wide-eyed.
It's true, as you say,
That it's been a long day,
But I just don't feel tired inside.

John Kitching

28

Under the stairs

I don't like the cupboard
Under the stairs,
It reminds me of caves
And dragons' lairs.

So I never look in
Once it is night,
In case I should get
A nasty fright.

I'm silly I know
'Cos it's only small
There wouldn't be room
For a dragon, at all.

But even in daytime
It gives me the scares
To go past the cupboard
Under the stairs.

Daphne Lister

Launderama

The clothes go bouncing up and down
the powder seethes and soaps
the load reverses and goes on
the light clicks off and stops.

The drier is as hot as fire
You fold your clothes away
cleaned of their rain and mud and mire
until another day.

Iain Crichton Smith

'I thought you liked your bath'

'I thought you liked your bath,' cried Daddy,
'Why are you shouting so?'

'I've still got my slippers on my feet;
I thought, perhaps, you'd like to know.'

He shook the slippers off his daughter,
And, grinning, laid her in the water.

Gregory Harrison

Stunning feat

I washed my feet last Thursday
    I scrubbed 'em again today
If I'm not very careful
    I'll wash them clean away.

John Rice

Billy's Bath

Billy was having a bath
Tra la
With a yodel, a yell and a laugh
Tra la
He swallowed the soap, which hung from a rope,
The whole cake, not even a half,
Tra la.

And he bibbled a bit, and dribbled a bit
Then a fountain of bubbles blew out,
Tra la.
And the big bubbles blew, and they spouted and grew,
Every time that he uttered a shout,
Tra la.
And they bounced down the stairs, and they took unawares
All the family sitting at tea,
Tra la.
And they spread over the table, and no one was able, to eat,
Because they couldn't see,
Tra la.
And they looked high and low, in the bubbles, like snow
For young Bill; they're still looking today,
Tra la.
And if you shine a bright light in the black of the night
You can see him there floating away,
Tra la.

Clive Riche

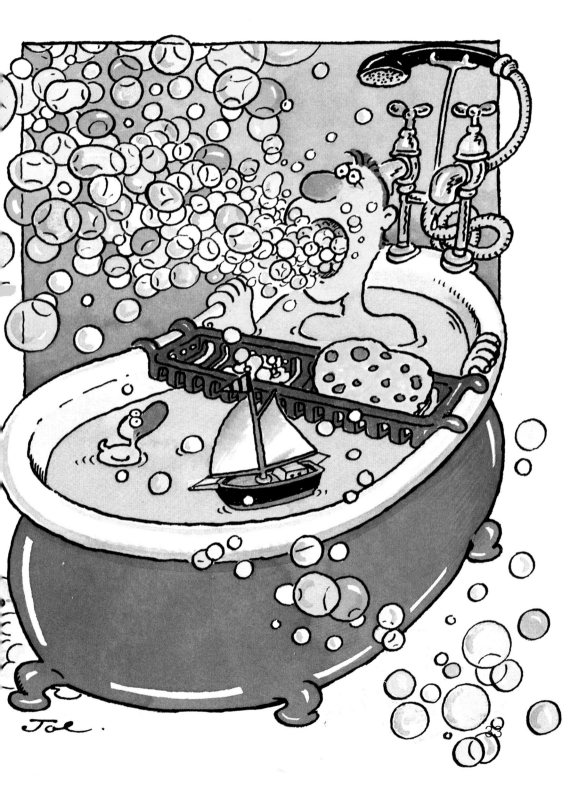

My uncle is a baronet

My uncle is a baronet,
He sleeps beside the hearth,
And likes to play the clarinet
While sitting in the bath.

Colin West

Two funny men

I know a man
Who's upside down,
And when he goes to bed
His head's not on the pillow. No!
His *feet* are there instead.

I know a man
Who's back to front,
The strangest man *I've* seen.
He can't tell where he's going
But he knows where he has been.

Spike Milligan

Space Spot

Twinkle, twinkle little star
    Up there in the blue.
How I wonder what you are,
    Are you Dr Who?

Max Fatchen

If stars were sweets

If stars were sweets
Then I would reach
Into the sky,
And I would try
To grab as many
To take back
And eat them, for comfort,
When the night
Was black
For lack
Of stars.

Clive Riche

36

Hot Water Bottles

It's comforting
    when winter's here
to have hot water bottles near
providing
they are good and stout
and do *not*
let the water out.
    There's nothing good
that can be said
of leaky bottles
    in the bed
not hot
    but cold and wet
            instead.

Peggy Dunstan

I play at sleep and then I raise

I play at sleep and then I raise
My legs up in the air;
He rushes to my bed and growls
Just like a grizzly bear.

I grope for grandpa's glasses
And drag them down his nose;
He makes a show of being cross
And gobbles up my toes.

Gregory Harrison

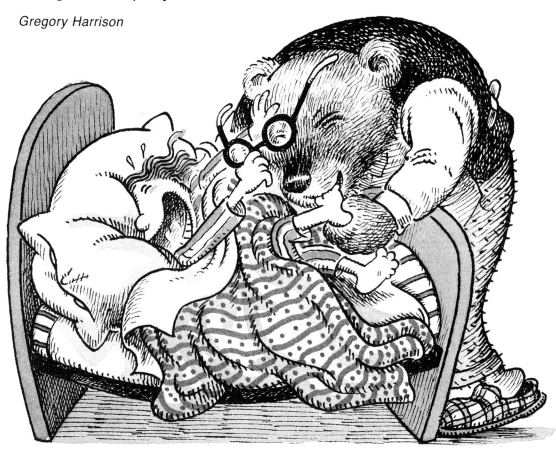

Bear

There was a boy
who almost saw
a bear inside
his bed.

O bear, what are
you looking for?
He almost went
and said;

And are you looking
for a boy
that's fat and nicely
fed?

But then he shut
his eyes, and thought
of other things
instead.

Jean Kenward

Counting sheep

They said,
'If you can't get to sleep
try counting sheep.'
I tried.
It didn't work.

They said,
'Still awake? Count rabbits, dogs
Or leaping frogs.'
I tried.
It didn't work.

They said,
'It's *very* late. Count rats,
or red-eyed bats!'
I tried.
It didn't work.

They said,
'Stop counting stupid sheep!
EYES CLOSED! DON'T PEEP!'
I tried
and fell asleep.

Wes Magee

41

Lullaby

Close your eyes gently
    And cuddle in
Keep yourself snug, a
    New day will begin.

Have pleasant dreams about
    Those things you love,
Sleep is an island
    Waiting above.

Night is a blanket
    Keeping you warm
If you close eyes you can
    Come to no harm.

Dreams are like journeys
    Drifting along,
Rest is a present
    Keeping you strong.

Alan Bold

Bump!

Things that go 'bump!' in the night,
Should not really give one a fright.
It's the hole in each ear
That lets in the fear,
That, and the absence of light!

Spike Milligan

Nightening

When you wake up at night
and it's dark and frightening,
don't be afraid –
turn on the lightening.

Michael Dugan

The old man of Peru

There was an old man of Peru,
Who dreamt he was eating his shoe.
    He woke in the night
    In a terrible fright,
And found it was perfectly true.

Anon.

Late for breakfast

Who is it hides my sandals when I'm trying to get dressed?
And takes away the hair brush that was lying on the chest?
I wanted to start breakfast before any of the others
But something's always missing or been borrowed by my
  brothers.
I think I'd better dress at night, and eat my breakfast too,
    Then when everybody's hurrying –
    I'll have nothing else to do.

Mary Dawson

I like soft-boiled eggs

I like soft-boiled eggs.
I like liver.
I like chicken legs
And jelly. See it shiver.

I like cabbage –
All kinds of greens.
I like sausages
And bubbling brown baked beans.

John Kitching

The sausage

The sausage is a cunning bird
With feathers long and wavy;
It swims about the frying pan
And makes its nest in gravy.

Anon.

Chips

They don't have any stones
They don't have any pips
They don't have any bones
That's why I like chips.

Julie Holder

Pepper and Salt

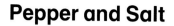

I peppered my fish and salted my chips
At supper the other night,
Then all of a sudden my fish gave a sneeze
And I got a terrible fright.

Barbara Ireson

Betsy Pud

Did you ever come upon
Betsy Pud?
She ate much more
than a nice girl should –
You never have seen
the like of it –
she ate until
her garters split.

Whether her work
was best or worst
she always stood
in the lunch queue, first.

Whether they liked
her ways, or not,
she licked her plate
to the last, small drop;

And then, one morning –
bless my soul! –
she wolfed the whole
of a treacle roll!

Yes, every morsel,
(wasn't it rude?)
went into the tummy
of Betsy Pud;

There wasn't a fraction,
wasn't a crumb
for anyone else
who cared to come,

And Betsy swelled
at such a rate, OH!
She up and burst
like a baked potato!

What a disaster!
What a sin!
They had to bring
the hoover in,

And off she went in it.
Nobody should
be quite so greedy
as Betsy Pud.

Jean Kenward

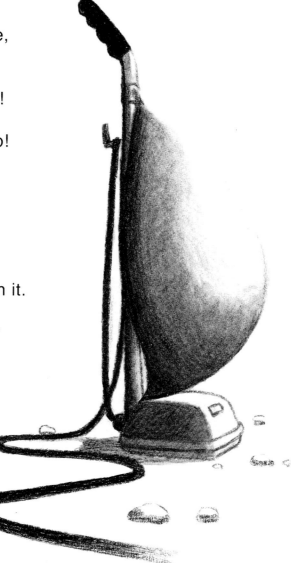

When Betty eats spaghetti

When Betty eats spaghetti,
She slurps, she slurps, she slurps.
And when she's finished slurping,
She burps, she burps, she burps.

Colin West

52

If your roly poly jelly

If your roly poly jelly
    Falls splat on the floor,
Take your shoes and socks off
    And kick it out the door!

John Rice

The HICCUP

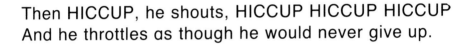

He keeps himself hidden,
An invisible man,
No one knows where he comes from
Or how he began.

But how he can travel
Like a sleek racing-boat
When he's in his position
To shoot down your throat.

Then HICCUP, he shouts, HICCUP HICCUP HICCUP
And he throttles as though he would never give up.

One youngster was eating
All through the school dance.
He stayed in a corner
A-waiting his chance.

He watched her devouring
The food – peck, peck, peck –
Then he rushed like a rocket
And whirled round her neck.

Then HICCUP, he shouts, HICCUP HICCUP HICCUP
And he throttles as though he would never give up.

On another occasion
An infant I knew
Was told if she ate meat
To be sure to chew.

Well, she did that, but when
She wanted a drink
She gulped it so quickly
He was there in a wink.

Then HICCUP, he shouts, HICCUP HICCUP HICCUP
And he throttles as though he would never give up.

There is one way to beat him.
Just one, that is all,
And the best time to learn it
Is when you are small.

He cannot get near you
If you eat as you should.
So, get rid of the Hiccup
And don't BOLT your food.

Or HICCUP, he'll shout, HICCUP HICCUP HICCUP
And he'll throttle as though he would never give up.

Alan Bold

Banana Talk

Bananas, said his mother, are curved and yellow.
They come in great bunches
like the hands of a gorilla.

Where do they come from? he asked her.

Jungles, she answered, where there are spiders.
The spiders are big and hairy
like gorillas' hands.

And do you like them? he asked.

They slide down, she murmured, pulpy-soft
and taste like pear-drops and scented wool.
They were my favourites.

And they're yellow? he asked quietly.

The skins are yellow.
They deepen blotchily towards brown
and they're ready to eat.

Do you eat the skins?

The skins are beautiful, she said, to look at.
But they're the worst part of bananas.
You peel them off, throw them away,
and what you're left with, you eat.
It's white, and pithy-looking
like the inside of a conker-wrapper.

And what about the skins? he asked,
thinking yellow.

Men slip up on them, she said lightly.
And you have a good laugh.

Brian Jones

Party Piece

I love to go to parties
And spoil all the fun
By sitting in the custard tarts
And throwing buttered buns.

John Jenkin

Spell

To be said to a balloon being blown up

    Love me, you'll grow fat and fly,
    Hate me, you'll grow thin and die.
    Sail, O sail the windy sky!
        Hate me, thinner,
        Nothing for dinner;
        Love me, fatter,
        Butter and batter.
    Fatter, fatter, fatter, fatter –

Ian Serraillier

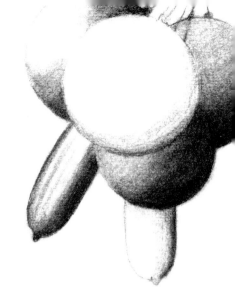

BANG

Happy Birthday Card

H appy birthday, all of us say
A nd may you have a lovely day.
P lenty of nice dreams!
P resents and ice creams!
Y ucky buns!
B est of fun!
I nteresting invitations!
R ailway stations!
T elly and trips!
H amburgers and chips! *BUT*
D o get a cough (if) –
A nd I hope your knees fall off (if)
Y ou forget mine

Rony Robinson

Ways of the week

Sunday
Good-to-be-done day.

Monday
Rabbit and gun day.

Tuesday
Fall, blackened bruise day.

Wednesday
Clucking old hen's day.

Thursday
Purring, warm fur's day.

Friday
Can't-make-me-cry day.

Saturday
Just doesn't matter day.

John Kitching

Mystery Story

A morning in May,
And we rolled up to school
In the usual way.

Well no, we didn't really,
Because the school wasn't there;
We rolled up to where
The school *had been*.
There was nothing.
It had all gone
And there wasn't a clue:
No hole, no scar,
Just a buttercup field
And a couple of larks
Singing over it.

You'd have thought there might be
A lot of cheering from the kids,
But there wasn't.
They all just stood around
Wondering,
Not even talking much.

Eric Finney

Another Day

Boys shout,
Girls giggle,
Pencils write,
Squiggle squiggle.
Get it wrong,
Cross it out,
Bell's gone,
All out!

Balls bounce,
Hands clap,
Skipping ropes,
Slap slap.
Hand-stands,
By the wall,
Sara Williams,
Best of all.
Boys fight,
Girls flee,
Teacher's gone
And spilt
His tea.
Clatter bang!
Big din,
Whistle goes,
All in!

All quiet,
No sound,
Hear worms,
Underground.
Chalk squeaks,
Clock creeps,
Head on desk,
Boy sleeps.

Home time,
Glory be,
Mum's got,
Chips for tea.
Warm fire,
Full belly,
Sit down,
Watch telly.

Bed time,
Creep away,
Dream until,
Another day.

John Cunliffe

The Summer Sun

Oh,
The sun shines bright
In the summer,
And the breeze is soft
As a sigh.

Oh,
The days are long
In the summer,
And the sun is king
Of the sky.

Wes Magee

Up on the Downs

Up on the Downs
Up on the Downs
A skylark flutters
        And the fox barks shrill,
Brown rabbit scutters
        And a hawk hangs still,
Up on the Downs
Up on the Downs
With butterflies jigging
        Like costumed clowns.

Here in the Hills
Here in the Hills
The long grass flashes
        And the sky seems vast,
Rock lizard dashes
        And a crow flies past,
Here in the Hills
Here in the Hills
With bumble bees buzzing
        Like high-speed drills.

Wes Magee

The sea

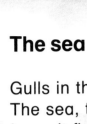

Gulls in the air –
The sea, the sea!
I saw it first!
The sea.

Shell at my ear –
The sea, the sea!
I heard it first!
The sea.

Sand in my shoe –
The sea, the sea!
I felt it first!
The sea.

Spade in my hand –
The sea, the sea!
I splashed it first!
The sea.

Cold on my toe –
The sea, the sea!
I paddled first!
The sea.

John Kitching

Sea Song

Sea-shell, sea-shell,
Murmuring sand,
Murmuring sand.

Sea-shell, sea-shell,
Far-away land,
Far-away land.

Sea-shell, sea-shell,
Sing in my hand,
Sing in my hand.

Sea-shell, sea-shell,
I'll understand,
You'll understand.

James Kirkup

69

The Dolphin

On a beach in the morning
The sea green and blue
A young child was resting:
The same age as you.

From a spot near a towel
A whispering came
Like the rustle of leaves
Or a voice in a dream.

Where the ripples were circling
A dolphin appeared
And said, 'Come down with me'.
And then – DISappeared.

The child entered softly
And reached the sea-floor
And saw not a sign
Of the golden sea-shore.

There were molluscs in sea-shells
Anemones too,
And more fish than the child
Had observed in the zoo.

On the back of the dolphin
The child wished and watched
How the fish gather round
As the fish-eggs are hatched.

Faster and faster
The dolphin progressed
And they passed near to China
As they streaked from the West.

And there there were goldfish
As large as your knee,
And twenty-five pandas
Asleep by the sea.

In India fish had
The most wonderful marks
(But they missed out Australia
Because of the sharks).

At the end of the journey
They were back near the beach
Where they talked of their trip
With bubbles for speech.

Then the child swam back strongly
To the spot on the sand
And covered up eyes
With the back of a hand.

In an hour the child woke up
In bed, it would seem,
Do you think that it happened
Or was it a dream?

Alan Bold

We've got a Wa Wa

We've got a Wa Wa in our house
Squelchy as an octopus and scratchy as a mouse
Slippy and slurpy
Ever-so dirty
Wet and slimy
And its eyes – cor blimey!
Nose all runny
Cheeks all funny
Claws all queer
And its tail – oh dear!
We've got a Wa Wa comes at night,
Waits in my bedroom to give my dad a fright.

We've got a Wa Wa only I can see
Comes out at night but just for me
Nasty and nobbly
Wibbly and wobbly
Sloshy and slow
And its teeth – oh no!
Lips all lumpy
Bum all bumpy
Ears all runny
And its horns – oh mummy!
We've got a Wa Wa, come and see,
Scares my dad, but is very nice to me.

I'm going to bring my Wa Wa to school,
Even if pets are against the rule.
Squiggly and squelchy
Bubbly and belchy
Doesn't wash
And its roar – oh gosh!
Legs all floppy
Feet all soppy
Name you'll find out
Be careful – mind out!
I've got a Wa Wa, pleased to meet you,
If you're nasty, my Wa Wa'll eat you!

Rony Robinson

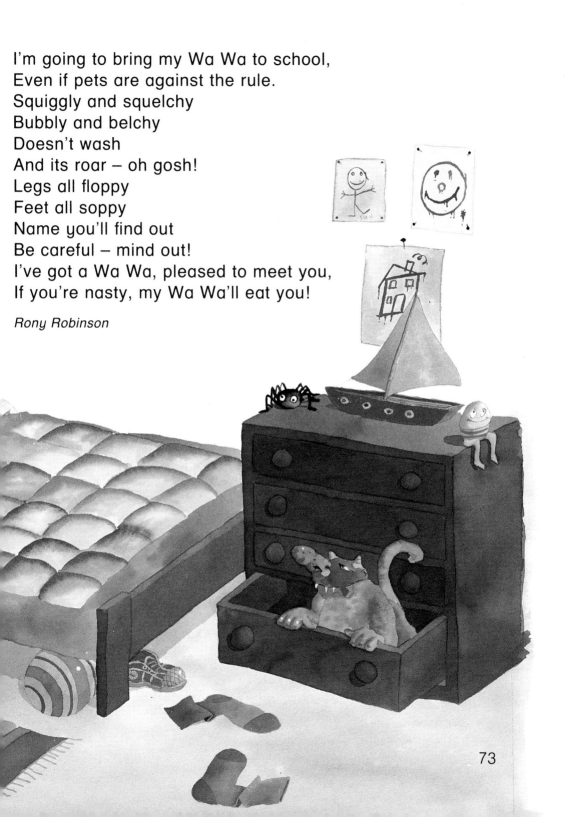

The Sick Young Dragon

'What can I do?' young dragon cried.
'Although I've simply tried and tried,
It doesn't matter how hard I blow,
I cannot get my fire to go!'

'Open your mouth!' his mother said.
'It's no wonder! Your throat's not red.
Your scales are cold. You must be ill.
I think you must have caught a chill.'

The doctor came. He looked and said,
'You'll need a day or two in bed.
Your temperature's down. No doubt
That's the reason your fire's gone out.

'Just drink this petrol. Chew these nails.
They'll help you to warm up your scales.
Just take it easy. Watch T V,
You'll soon be right as rain, you'll see.'

Young dragon did as he was told
And soon his scales stopped feeling cold.
He sneezed some sparks. His face glowed bright.
He coughed and set the sheets alight.

'Oh dear!' he cried. 'I've burnt the bed!'
'It doesn't matter,' his mother said.
'Those sheets were old. Go out and play.
Just watch where you breathe fire today!'

John Foster

74

Conversation

I'm big and strong,
The giant says,
Big, strong and tough.
And with one puff
I could blow you along
Like a fragment of fluff.

With a huff huff great big puff
He's big and strong and he's ever so tough.

I'm small and slight,
The dancer says,
Small, slight and fleet.
And with my feet
I could dance all tonight
And make even you sweet.

With her fleet fleet dainty feet
She's small and slight and she's ever so sweet.

Look at my arm,
The giant says,
Muscles like steel.
There, can you feel
All the danger and harm?
It's not nice but it's real.

Yes they're real real very real
Danger and harm in those muscles of steel.

Now I can see,
The dancer says,
Just what you are.
Will you look there,
There past the tree
That rests under the star?

Just what you are, giant, just what you are
Look at the tree that rests under the star.

Where have you gone,
The giant says,
Why did you go?
I'll never know
Now till the dawn
How a friend becomes foe.

You'll never know, giant, you'll never know
Just how a new friend becomes an old foe.

Alan Bold

So Big!

The dinosaur, an ancient beast,
I'm told, was very large.
His eyes were big as billiard balls,
His stomach, a garage.
He had a huge and humping back,
A neck as long as Friday.
I'm glad he lived so long ago
And didn't live in my day!

Max Fatchen

Granny boot

Granny in her bed one night
Heard a little squeak!
And then a little
peck-peck-peck
Like something with a beak
Then something that went Binkle-Bonk
Ickle-tickle-toot
And all of it was coming
From inside Grandma's boot!
Then the boot began to *hop*
It went into the hall
And then from deep inside the boot
Came a Tarzan call
The sound of roaring lions
The screech of a cockatoo
Today that boot is in a cage
Locked in the London Zoo.

Spike Milligan

Geraldine Giraffe

The
longest
ever
woolly
scarf
was
worn
by
Geraldine
Giraffe.
Around
her
neck
the
scarf
she
wound,
but
still
it
trailed
upon
the
ground.

Colin West

Glow-worm

I know a worried glow-worm,
I wonder what the matter is?
He seems so glum and gloomy,
Perhaps he needs new batteries!

Colin West

The Stork

This is the tale of a poor old stork
Whose end was full of gloom;
For in a moment of carelessness
He went to meet his doom.

When poised in thought, one foot aloft,
While learning how to beg,
He went and quite forgot himself –
And raised the *other* leg.

Carey Blyton

Hippopotamuses

Hippopotamuses never
Put on boots in rainy weather.
To slosh in mud up to their ears
Brings them great joy and merry tears.
Their pleasure lies in being messed up
They just won't play at being dressed up.
In fact a swamp is heaven plus
If you're a hippopotamus.

Arnold Spilka

Though hippos weigh at least a tonne

Though hippos weigh at least a tonne,
They love to wade and wallow,
They never sink.
I sometimes think
A hippo must be hollow!

Doug Macleod

83

Circus Elephant

Does the Elephant remember
In the grey light before dawn,
Old noises of the jungle
In mornings long gone?

Does the Elephant remember
The cry of hungry beasts;
The Tiger and the Leopard,
The Lion at his feasts?

Do his mighty eardrums listen
For the thunder of the feet
Of the Buffalo and Zebra
In the dark and dreadful heat?

Does His Majesty remember,
Does he stir himself and dream
Of the long-forgotten music
Of a long-forgotten stream?

Kathryn Worth

85

Tiger

I'm a tiger
Striped with fur
Don't come near
Or I might Grrr
Don't come near
Or I might growl
Don't come near
Or I might
BITE!

Mary Ann Hoberman

86

There was a young lady of Riga

There was a young lady of Riga,
Who rode with a smile on a tiger,
They returned from the ride
With the lady inside,
And the smile on the face of the tiger.

Anon

If

If I were a bear, a grizzly bear,
I wouldn't politely pull, I'd tear,
and rip and growl and grunt and scowl
and make all the squirrels stare.

If I were a bear, a brown teddy-bear,
I wouldn't just sit around in a chair,
but snuggle and huddle and comfort and cuddle
any children who might be there.

Malcolm Carrick

Barney and Fred

Fancy eating your bed
Like the guinea pigs Barney and Fred
Who nibble away
Wood shavings and hay.

I should never feel
Like making my house a meal
And gnawing the wood
To do my teeth good.

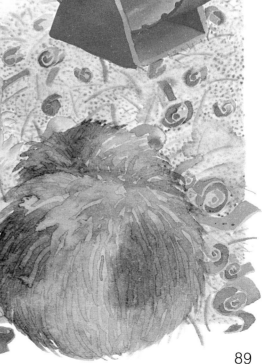

I never met anyone yet
Who ate the floor and carpet
Except, as I said,
Barney and Fred.

Stanley Cook

The Gerbil

The gerbil stands up
Crouching like a kangaroo
Ready to hop;
To him the children he sees
Seem tall as trees;
His paws clutch
The teacher's hand
That stretches like a branch
Above the sand
Of the tiny desert
In his hutch.

Stanley Cook

Dogs

Dogs big, dogs small
Dogs short, dogs tall
Dogs fat, dogs thin
Dogs that make a dreadful din

Dogs smooth, dogs hairy
Dogs friendly, dogs scary
Dogs brown, dogs white
Dogs that bark all through the night.

Dogs that run, dogs that walk
Dogs that make you think they'll talk,
Dogs awake, dogs asleep
Dogs for the blind, dogs for the sheep.

The best of all the dogs I know
Goes with me everywhere I go.

John Kitching

Our Cats

Our cats stay out all night,
Moonlighting.
You should hear them spitting
And fighting!

At breakfast time they come in
Purring
And curl on chairs; no hint of
Stirring!

Then when it's dark they're off
Exploring
While thunder growls and gales
Are roaring!

When we're tucked-up in bed
Sound-sleeping
They're out there ... in the darkness
... creeping!

Wes Magee

92

My name is Supermouse

My name is Supermouse
I live in a Superhouse
I do as I please
I eat Supercheese
I chase Superrats
And I frighten nine lives
Out of all Supercats.

John Kitching

The kitten

The trouble with a kitten is
THAT
Eventually it becomes a
CAT.

Ogden Nash

Black Cat

A cat as black
As blackest coal
Is out upon
His midnight stroll.
His steps are soft,
His walk is slow,
His eyes are gold,
They flash and glow.
And so I run
And so I duck,
I do not need
His black-cat luck.

Jack Prelutsky

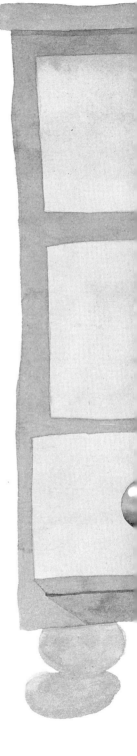

The Witch! The Witch!

The Witch! The Witch!
Don't let her get you!
Or your Aunt wouldn't know you
      the next time she met you!

Eleanor Farjeon

96

Witch, Witch

'Witch, witch, where do you fly?'...
'Under the clouds and over the sky.'

'Witch, witch, what do you eat?'...
'Little black apples from Hurricane Street.'

'Witch, witch, what do you drink?'...
'Vinegar, blacking and good red ink.'

'Witch, witch, where do you sleep?'...
'Up in the clouds where pillows are cheap.'

Rose Fyleman

The Witch's Brew

Into my pot there now must go
Leg of lamb and a green frog's toe.

Old men's socks and dirty jeans,
A rotten egg and cold baked beans.

> Hubble bubble at the double
> Cooking pot stir up some trouble.

One dead fly and a wild wasp's sting,
The eye of a sheep and the heart of a King.

A stolen jewel and mouldy salt
And for good flavour a jar of malt.

> Hubble bubble at the double
> Cooking pot stir up some trouble.

Wing of bird and head of mouse,
Screams and howls from a haunted house.

And don't forget the pint of blood
Or the sardine tin and the clod of mud.

> Hubble bubble at the double
> Cooking pot stir up some trouble.

Wes Magee

BEST
MOUSE
HEADS

Joe

Hallowe'en

Bring a candle!
   Bring a light –
it must be Hallowe'en
   tonight!

I saw a pixie
   small and fine
dancing
   on the washing line...

I saw a witch
   go riding high
on her broomstick
   through the sky...

I saw a giant
   ten feet wide
with half a dozen
   ships inside...

I saw a fairy
   like a dream
top the milk
   and sip the cream...

I saw a goblin
   plump and brown
turn the church clock
   upside down!

Come as quickly
as you can —
I saw the back
of a bogy man!

Jean Kenward

Haunted House

There's a house upon the hilltop
We will not go inside
For that is where the witches live,
Where ghosts and goblins hide.

Tonight they have their party,
All the lights are burning bright,
But oh we will not go inside
The haunted house tonight.

The demons there are whirling
And the spirits swirl about.
They sing their songs to Hallowe'en.
'Come join the fun,' they shout.

But we do not want to go there
So we run with all our might
And oh we will not go inside
The haunted house tonight.

Jack Prelutsky

The goblin

There's a goblin as green
As a goblin can be
Who is sitting outside
And is waiting for me.

When he knocked on my door
And said softly, 'Come play.'
I answered, 'No thank you,
Now, please, go away.'

But the goblin as green
As a goblin can be
Is still sitting outside
And is waiting for me.

Jack Prelutsky

Ghost

I saw a ghost
that stared and stared
And I stood still
and acted scared.
But that was just
a big pretend.
I knew that ghost...
... it was my friend.

Jack Prelutsky

The Hidebehind

Have you seen the Hidebehind?
I don't think you will, mind you,
because as you're running through the dark
the Hidebehind's behind you.

Michael Rosen

104

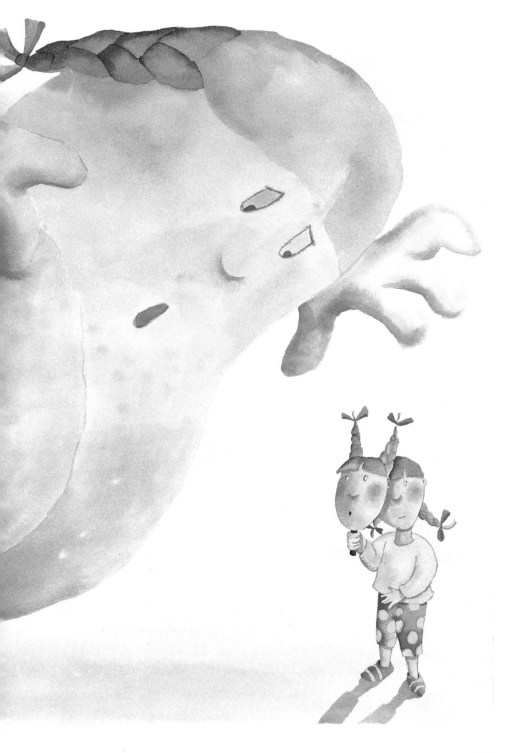

Dark Windy Night

When I was out walking
One dark windy night
I heard something behind me
One dark windy night
A footstep, a whisper
One dark windy night
A shadow before me
One dark windy night
Moonlight behind me
One dark windy night.
I shivered, I shook,
I did get a fright
When I was out walking
One dark windy night.

Anne English

Wind Song

When the wind blows
The quiet things speak.
Some whisper, some clang,
Some creak.

Grasses swish.
Treetops sigh.
Flags slap
and snap at the sky.
Wires on poles
Whistle and hum.
Ashcans roll.
Windows drum.

When the wind goes –
suddenly
then,
the quiet things
are quiet again.

Lilian Moore

It ain't gonna rain no more, no more

It ain't gonna rain no more, no more,
It ain't gonna rain no more;
How in the heck can I wash my neck
If it ain't gonna rain no more?

Anon.

Whether the weather be fine

Whether the weather be fine,
Or whether the weather be not,
Whether the weather be cold,
Or whether the weather be hot,
We'll weather the weather
Whatever the weather
Whether we like it or not.

Anon.

Welcoming Winter

Knock knock!
Who's there?
– It's a penguin hopping
up the stair.

Knock, knock!
Who's here?
– The child who comes but
once a year.

Knock, knock!
Who's this?
– Listen to the
kettle hiss.

Knock, knock!
Who's that?
– It's the snowman
on the Welcome mat.

James Kirkup

Sir Winter

I heard Sir Winter coming.
He crept out of his bed
and rubbed his thin and freezing hands:
'I'll soon be up!' he said.

'I'll shudder at the keyhole
and rattle at the door,
I'll strip the trees of all their leaves
and strew them on the floor;

'I'll harden every puddle
that Autumn thinks is his –
I'll lay a sparkling quilt of snow
on everything that is!

'I'll bring a load of darkness
as large as any coal,
and drive my husky dogs across
the world, from pole to pole.

'Oho! How you will shiver!'
And then I heard him say:
'But in the middle of it all
'I'll give you
                    CHRISTMAS DAY!'

Jean Kenward

A Good Idea for Wintry Weather

At breakfast in the dark I pop
my dad's hat over the teapot
so that his head shall be hot
though the full buses pass his stop.

Libby Houston

Calling

   The sky is grey
And snow is falling.
The winter winds are
   Calling, calling.

   Outside, it's wild.
Dad's car is stalling.
Next door my friends are
   Calling, calling.

   Sliding, sledging
And, oh, snowballing!
December's pleasures
   Calling, calling.

Wes Magee

Snowman

Roly poly icy snow,
We're trying to build
A Snowman Joe.

We press and punch
And squeeze and pound
Until his body's thick and round;
And on the top to make him tall
We slam an icy, tingling ball;
Then on his head with bits of stone
In finger-tips of aching bone
We make some ears,
A mouth, a nose
And two dark eyes that will not close;
With bits of coal from feet to throat
We button up his winter coat.

But, oh, our hands.
With moans and cries
We thrust them in between our thighs.

Gregory Harrison

Paws

My gloves are woollen paws
My mother knitted for me
While we were watching
T.V. after tea.

They keep me as warm
In the winter cold
As the fur of the big white bears
Who live in the ice and snow.

Stanley Cook

Robin

If on a frosty morning
the robin redbreast calls
his waistcoat red and burning
like a beggar at your walls

throw breadcrumbs on the grass for him
when the ground is hard and still
for in his breast there is a flame
that winter cannot kill.

Iain Crichton Smith

Spring Song

Have you ever seen
    such green, such green?
Have you ever seen
    such blue
as the woods in April
    when they blink
and a bit of the sky
    looks through?
And the light – the light
    is tiny and bright
in every blob
    of dew?
Have you ever seen
    such green, such green?
Have you ever seen
    such blue?

Jean Kenward

The river

Who lives forever?
The river.
Who sees all weather?
The river.
Who rushes past kings, with their crowns, swords and rings,
Who bubbles and sings?
The river.

Who goes all places?
The river.
Who sees all faces?
The river.
Who dawdles, who gushes, over boulders and rushes,
Who pulls and who pushes?
The river.

Clive Riche

The sun wakes up

The sun wakes up
Yes, the sun wakes up.

The sun it smiles
Yes, the sun it smiles.

The wind it blows
Yes, the wind it blows.

The clouds come over
Yes, the clouds come over.

The rain falls down
Yes, the rain falls down.

The earth dries up
Yes, the earth dries up.

The sun lies down
Yes, the sun lies down.

The dark moves in
Yes, the dark moves in.

The moon looks up
Yes, the moon looks up.

The night lies still
Yes, the night lies still.

The old folk die
Yes, the old folk die.

The sun wakes up
Yes, the sun wakes up.

John Rice

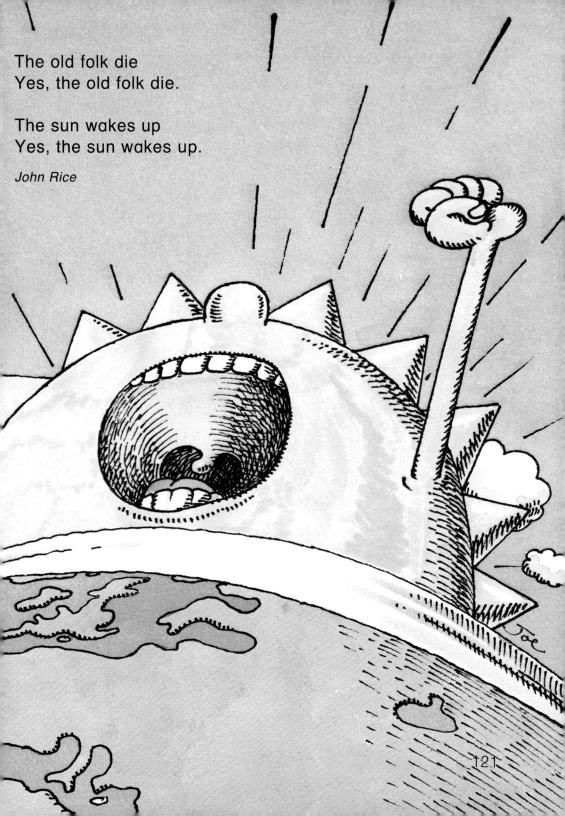

Sad Things

A puddle that looks like
A rainbow that's drowned,
Not taking home
The stray kitten you've found,
Losing a treasure,
Finding it broken,
Angry words
You wish you'd not spoken.

Mad Things

Running wild with the wind
When it's blowing wild,
Pretending to be
A different child,
Eating the snowflakes
As they fall from the sky,
Getting the giggles
Without knowing why.

Scary Things

Under the bed
After saying goodnight,
Getting stuck in a sweater
That's much too tight,
Getting lost at the fair
or the shops or the zoo,
Feeling something
With lots of legs
Crawling on you.

Glad Things

With your head and your hands
Thinking something to make,
Blowing out with one breath
All the candles on cake,
To rescue a bird
And watch it fly free,
Mum saying 'yes you can'
Not just 'we'll see'.

Julie Holder

124

Index of First Lines

Acknowledgements

The following poems are being published for the first time in this anthology and appear by permission of their author unless otherwise stated: Alan Bold: 'Lullaby', 'The Hiccup', 'The Dolphin', and 'Conversation' all © 1984 Alan Bold. Stanley Cook: 'Paws' © 1984 Stanley Cook. John Cunliffe: 'Another Day' © 1984 John Cunliffe. Eric Finney: 'Mystery Story' © 1984 Eric Finney. John Foster: 'The sick young dragon' © 1984 John Foster. Gregory Harrison: 'A clear day and a yellow sun', ' "I thought you liked your bath," cried Daddy', 'Snowman', and 'I play at sleep and then I raise' all © 1984 Gregory Harrison. Julie Holder: 'Chips' and 'Sad things, Mad things, Scary things, Glad things' both © 1984 Julie Holder. Brian Jones: 'Banana talk' © 1984 Brian Jones. Jean Kenward: 'Betsy Pud', 'Hallowe'en', 'Sir Winter', and 'Spring song' all © 1984 Jean Kenward. James Kirkup: 'Sea song' and 'Welcoming winter' both © 1984 James Kirkup. John Kitching: 'Snore-a-bye daddy', 'I had no friends at all', 'I don't want to go up to bed', 'I like soft-boiled eggs', 'Ways of the week', 'The sea', 'Dogs', and 'Supermouse' all © 1984 John Kitching. Wes Magee: 'The digging song', 'Counting sheep', 'The summer sun', 'Up on the Downs', 'Our cats', 'The witch's brew', and 'Calling' all © 1984 Wes Magee. Seamus Redmond: 'Flutter By' © 1984 Seamus Redmond. John Rice: 'Skipping rhyme', 'If your roly poly jelly', and 'The sun wakes up' all © 1984 John Rice. Clive Riche: 'These are the clothes that my big brother wore', 'Paint on my fingers', 'Billy's bath', 'If stars were sweets', and 'The river' all © 1984 Clive Riche. Rony Robinson: 'Happy Birthday Card' and 'We've got a Wa Wa' both © 1984 Rony Robinson. Michael Rosen: 'Humpty Dumpty went to the moon' © 1984 Michael Rosen. Iain Crichton Smith: 'Launderama' © 1984 Iain Crichton Smith.

The Editor and Publisher wish to thank the following for permission to reprint copyright poems in this anthology. Although every effort has been made to contact copyright holders a few have been impossible to trace. If they contact the Publisher, correct acknowledgement will be made in future editions.

Dorothy Aldis: 'I have to have it' from *All Together*. Copyright 1925–1928, 1934, 1939, 1952, renewed 1953–1956, 1962, 1967 by Dorothy Aldis. Reprinted by permission of G.P. Putnam's Sons. Carey Blyton: 'The Stork' from *Bananas in Pyjamas*. Reprinted by permission of Faber & Faber Ltd. Malcolm Carrick: 'If' from *Once There Was a Boy and Other Stories* (Puffin Books 1975) p. 61. © Malcolm Carrick, 1965. Reprinted by permission of Penguin Books Ltd. Stanley Cook: 'Barney and Fred' and 'The Gerbil' from *Come Along*, published by the author; 'Crayoning' and 'At Sea in the House' are from *Come Along Again*, published by Kirklees and Calderdale NATE, Studley House, Egerton, Huddersfield. All reprinted by permission of the author. Mary Dawson: 'Late for Breakfast' from *Allsorts 2* compiled by Ann Thwaite, published by Macmillan. Reprinted by permission of the author. Michael Dugan: 'Nightening' from *My Old Dad*. Reprinted by permission of Ginn & Co., Ltd. Peggy Dunstan: 'Hot Water Bottles' from *In and Out the Window*. Reprinted by permission of Hodder & Stoughton Children's Books. Anne English: 'Dark Windy Night' from *All the year round* ed. S. McKellar, Evans. Eleanor Farjeon: 'The Witch! The Witch!' from *Silver Sand and Snow* (Michael Joseph). Reprinted by permission of David Higham Associates Ltd. Max Fatchen: 'Little John was not content'; 'Space Spot' and 'So Big!' from *Songs For My Dog and Other People*. © Max Fatchen, 1980; 'Clumsy' from *Wry Rhymes for Troublesome Times*. © Max Fatchen. 1983. Reprinted by permission of Penguin Books Ltd., and John Johnson Ltd. Rose Fyleman: 'Witch, Witch' from *Fifty-one New Nursery Rhymes*. © 1931, 1932 by Rose Fyleman. Reprinted by permission of The Society of Authors as the literary representative of the Estate of Rose Fyleman and of Doubleday & Co., Inc. Mary Ann Hoberman: 'You were the mother last time' from *Not Enough Bed for the Babies* and 'Tiger' from *Hello and Good-By*. Libby Houston: 'A Good Idea for Wintry Weather'. Reprinted by permission of the author. John Jenkin: 'Party Piece' from *More Stuff and Nonsense*, ed. Michael Dugan. Reprinted by permission of the author. Jean Kenward: 'Bear' from *Old Mister Hotchpotch* (Thornhill Press). Reprinted by permission of the author. Daphne Lister: 'Under the stairs' from *Gingerbread Pig and other Rhymes* (Carousel Books, 1980). All Rights Reserved. Reprinted by permission of Transworld Publishers Ltd. Doug Macleod: 'Though hippos weigh at least a tonne' from *More Stuff and Nonsense*, ed. Michael Dugan. Reprinted by permission of the author. Spike Milligan: 'Bump' from *The Little Pot-Boiler* (n.e. Star Books, 1979). Reprinted by permission of Spike Milligan Productions. 'Two Funny Men' and 'Granny Boot' from *Unspun Socks From a Chicken's Laundry*, published by Michael Joseph with M & J. Hobbs. Reprinted by permission of Michael Joseph Ltd. Lilian Moore: 'Sometimes' and 'Wind Song' from *I Feel the Same Way*. Reprinted by permission of the author. Ogden Nash: 'The kitten' from *Verses from 1929 on*. Copyright 1940 by The Curtis Publishing Company. First appeared in *The Saturday Evening Post*. The poem is published in the UK in *I wouldn't Have Missed It* (Andre Deutsch 1983). Reprinted by permission of Little, Brown & Company and Andre Deutsch. Jack Prelutsky: 'Black Cat', 'Haunted House', 'The Goblin', and 'Ghost' from *It's Halloween*. © 1977 Jack Prelutsky. Reprinted by permission of World's Work Ltd., and Greenwillow Books (A Division of William Morrow). John Rice: 'Stunning Feat'. Reprinted by permission of the author. Michael Rosen: 'The Hidebehind' from *Mind Your Own Business*. © 1974 by Michael Rosen. Reprinted by permission of Andre Deutsch and S.G. Phillips Inc. 'A busy day'. Reprinted by permission of the author. Ian Serraillier: 'Spell to be said to a balloon being blown up', © 1973 Ian Serraillier, from *I'll Tell You a Tale* (Puffin books 1976). Reprinted by permission of the author. Iain Crichton Smith: 'Robin'. Reprinted by permission of the author. Arnold Spilka: 'Hippopotamuses' from *A Lion I Can Do Without* (Walck, 1964). © by Arnold Spilka. Reprinted by permission of Frances Schwartz Literary Agency. Colin West: 'Cousin Jane', 'When Betty Eats Spaghetti', 'Geraldine Giraffe', and 'Glow-worm' from *Not To Be Taken Seriously*. 'My Uncle is a Baronet' from *A Step in the Wrong Direction*. Reprinted by permission of Hutchinson Publishing Group Ltd. Raymond Wilson: 'Questions'. Reprinted by permission of the author. Kathryn Worth: 'Circus Elephant' from *A Child's Treasury of Verse* (edited by E. Doan). Reprinted by permission of Hodder & Stoughton Children's Books. 'Pepper and Salt' is from *The Beaver Book of Funny Rhymes*, edited by Barbara Ireson.